The Chain Saw Dance

Other Works by David Budbill

Poetry
> *Pulp Cutters' Nativity*
> *From Down to the Village*
> *Barking Dog*

Plays
> *Knucklehead Rides Again*
> *Mannequins' Demise*

Short Stories
> *Snowshoe Trek to Otter River*

Novel
> *Bones on Black Spruce Mountain*

Children's Book
> *Christmas Tree Farm*

The Chain Saw Dance

by David Budbill

Introduction by Hayden Carruth

Drawings by Lois Eby

The Countryman Press
Woodstock, Vermont

Text Copyright © 1976, 1977 by David Budbill

The Cover Drawing, "After Goya," and other drawings, Copyright © 1977 by Lois Eby

All rights reserved. Except for brief passages quoted in a review, no part of this book may be reproduced in any form or by any means without permission in writing from the publisher.

Grateful acknowledgment is made to the Vermont Council on the Arts and the National Endowment for the Arts for grants which aided in the writing and production of this book and to *Longhouse*, *North Coast Poetry* and *Poetry Now* in which some of these poems first appeared.

The Chain Saw Dance was originally designed by the Laughing Bear Associates and printed at Northlight Studio Press in conjunction with Perennial Press, Montpelier, Vermont. The text was composed in 11 point Times Roman by Vermont Typographics. First published by The Crow's Mark Press, Johnson, Vermont, in 1977, it appeared for the first time under The Countryman Press imprint in 1983.

First Printing: February 1977
Second Printing: October 1977
Third Printing: March 1978
Fourth Printing: December 1979

Fifth Printing: August 1983
Sixth Printing: March 1988
Seventh Printing: August 1990
Eighth Printing: February 1991

ISBN 0-88150-012-7
Manufactured in the United States of America

He fell in love with his own country —
that's a funny thing, eh?

    Henry Miller
    The Colossus of Maroussi

Contents

Introduction 9
Hermie 13
Anson 16
Old Man Pike 20
Bill 21
Arnie 24
Jimmy 29
Envoy to Jimmy 32
Antoine 33
Bobbie 42
Doug 43
Envoy to Doug 46
Granny 47
Forrest 52
Requiem for a Hill Farm 53
Albert 55
The Two Old Guys at Albert's 57
Tom 60
Driving Home at Night 62
Appendix 64

Introduction

Anyone who is close to contemporary American writing is aware that something new is happening and has been happening for the past two or three years; longer than that in some places. I mean the emergence of the new regionalism. This isn't a good term for it, and I hope to think of a better one eventually. But whatever its name, the thing itself is evident — in the Southwest, in the Prairies, in Upstate New York and Northern New England, in many areas where writers and painters are turning to the values of place, of locality, in their search for new substance and impetus.

It is happening spontaneously. Many questions arise from it — not the least of them being what these artists are turning away from, and why — but so far the theoretical aspects have not been widely discussed. That will come. The point now is that a widespread need is beginning to express itself and to do so in terms of the cultural, social, historical, and even philosophical values attached to particular local environments.

Certainly David Budbill had no sense of belonging to a movement when he began to write his poems about Judevine and East Judevine a few years ago. He did it because he was dissatisfied with the poetry he had been writing up till then, and because he became aware, rather abruptly, that what he was really interested in was the place where he lived, the other people who lived there, and the exact quality of his and their lives. He began writing. And as he wrote, as he developed his ideas (his plan is for an extended sequence of poems, of which the present offering is no more than a preliminary glimpse) he saw that the poems he was making out of his affection for particular people and his admiration for a particular way of life still bore important implications for everyone.

Not that David is a native. In a sense he has no nativity, and I think in this he is typical of many young writers throughout the country. He found his place by coming to it from elsewhere, with many stops along the way: college, grad school, teaching, political activism, etc. His own experience even included a spell of preaching in a church in southeastern Ohio. Well, in a mobile society people move around. Moreover, much of the movement is random. But what seems pertinent today is that this movement, in spite of its randomness, is taking artists more and more toward distinct small localities, not toward the cosmopolitan centers that seemed so attractive when I was young.

Where is Judevine? In north central Vermont. You won't find it on the map though, because David has fictionalized it, as he has also fictionalized the people in his poems. Yet he has been absolutely faithful to the reality of his material, as I can testify personally because I live not far away. Even the name, Judevine, possesses historical actuality in this region. Incidentally, it is pronounced trisyllabically, as in its French form, *jeu de vin*.

Part of David's fidelity to his materials lies in the matter of speech. I remember long ago, a couple of years after I had first read the novels and stories of James Joyce, somebody played for me the record of Joyce reading passages from his work. I was thunderstruck. The guy was a mick! Of course, I had known he was a "literary Irishman," whatever that meant, but I had never made the connection between Joyce and my Irish neighbors, though for years I had patronized Flannagan's saloon on 47th Street in Chicago. After that, with the lilt and whine of Irish in my ear, even though I couldn't imitate it properly I could read every sentence by Joyce with doubled understanding and appreciation.

Not many people know the speech of Judevine, which is, granted, a very small corner of the world. Yet that speech, its tone and cadence, is important, and perhaps some readers who have never heard it can at least imagine it if I describe its general characteristics. Basically it is Down East Yankee, as spoken from the Green Mountains to the coast of Maine and southward to Long Island Sound. But it is overlaid with the more gutteral, shortened accent of the Champlain Valley. Interested readers can see the difference by referring to the *Linguistic Atlas of New England* and the stories of Rowland E. Robinson. In addition, the speech of Judevine is heavily influenced by French Canadian, especially by certain turns of phrase that have been imported into English from the Joual (patois) of Quebec.

To transcribe dialect in standard orthography is always difficult, but I think David has done pretty well. He has caught the ordinary speech of Judevine, in its several levels of literacy and illiteracy, accurately and with enough linguistic precision to permit readers whose ears are sensitive to sound it. The case of French-Canadian dialect is more difficult still, however. A really accurate representation of French-Canadian English in the normal alphabet would be unreadable. Finally the case of Granny, in the poem bearing her name for its title, is utterly impossible. David and I spent many hours trying to score her magnificent wailing so that readers might not only understand it but appreciate its verbal qualities; but no system of notation, either musical or orthographic, can do the job. The poem must be heard. Consequently we hope to distribute a tape of David reading this and other poems with at least a few copies of this booklet. I wish we had money enough to do it with them all. For readers who must rely on the printed text alone we have appended a literal transcription of Granny's monologues at the end.

As for quality, I believe I should let the poems speak for themselves, as they will and do. Obviously what David Budbill is doing, what other poets like him are doing, is new. It departs from the contemporary norms of poetic composition as taught in our "creative writing schools" in a number of respects. Nevertheless, to my mind David's poems do conform, decidedly, to the basic esthetic criteria: balance, harmony, dynamism, integrity, concreteness, and the rest. And they are certainly effective and moving. I believe as well that they are important, both to poetry and to the changed sense of ourselves that we Americans must acquire if we are to reform our tottering society and survive. With these values in mind, I recommend David Budbill's poems heartily to the attention of all readers.

Hayden Carruth
5 March 1976

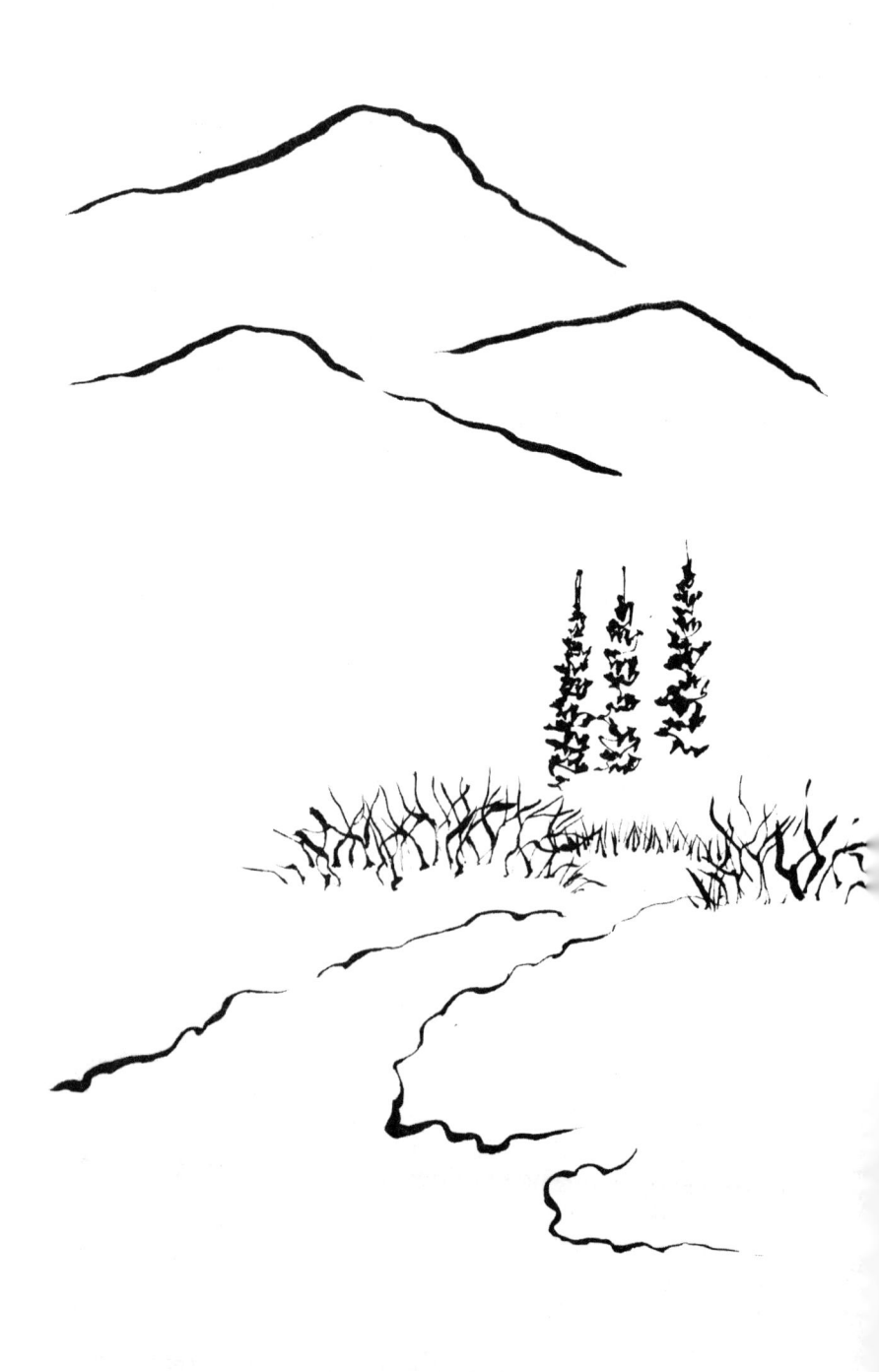

Hermie

Hermie Newcome lived in a bread truck on the edge
of Bear Swamp.
The bread truck is still there
with a spruce tree through the roof and the remains
of his last pig pen.
He had a bunk up front where the seats used to be
so in the morning he could wake up and look out
the windshield at the day.
There was a little wood stove in the back.
Hermie brought the stove wood in
through the rear doors so he wouldn't have to
lug it through his bedroom.
There was a table and a chair
and some crates for cupboards.
It was always neat in there.
It was a good place and cozy.
Hermie didn't need anything big as a bus.

His woman, Florence, was an Indian from New York.
Before he lived in the bread truck, they had a shack
next to the Dunn Hill cemetery and before that
they lived on Hermie's family place
on the Aiken Pond road up from the schoolhouse

where I used to live.
But one night while they were still at the homeplace,
Hermie got pissed at something, nobody knows what,
and flew into a rage, which he did about twice a week,
but this time went too far and lit both house and barn
and watched them burn.
When the neighbors came Hermie was out in the snow,
in the dooryard stomping and screaming,
"Burn! Goddamnit!
Burn! you wuthless place.
You never was no goddamn good!"

Nobody could ever be quite sure when Hermie was drunk.
He acted crazy all the time.
There's nothing left of the Newcome place now,
only the springbox. Those tamarack boards
will last forever.

Then they moved over to the shack by the cemetery.
Hermie liked it there,
said it was the first place he ever lived
where he had decent neighbors.

Antoine tells about going past there on a Saturday night
and seeing
Hermie and Florence dancing with the chain saw going
in the middle of the floor.
Hermie and Florence'd get drunk,
then Hermie would adjust the carburetor on the saw
so it would run too rich
so it would sputter and bounce with a rhythm
worthy of a good musician.
Then they'd sing and dance
to the music of the saw.

Hermie could cut pulp like a son-of-a-bitch;
he could bull and jam when he wanted to,
but that wasn't very often.
Everybody said he was worthless.
Hiram still says
his mother should of knocked him in the head when he was born
and spent the money on some grain to raise a pig.

Hermie never did anybody any harm;
in fact the night he burnt the homeplace
he was sure to get Florence and the cats out
before he struck the match.

He burnt the cemetery place too.
That's when Florence left him, went back
to the reservation or to Morrisville.
I don't know where.

Then he moved alone into the bread truck in the swamp.
Hermie spent his life looking for the perfect place.
That's what all those fires were about.
And in the end he found that place.
The bread truck wouldn't burn.

Anson

Anson was born on the place next door, half a mile away.

About ten years ago the University took part of the Boynton
                place for taxes.
(The University, by the way, has been delinquent on the taxes
                ever since.)
Not long after that the Boyntons sold out, but Anson came back
                a few years ago
with a French wife and two sons to farm his home.
He rented from the owner, a chiropractor in California.
Anson sold out last spring. The bank wouldn't loan him money
                for machinery
because he didn't own the place and because
the chiropractor wouldn't give him a long term lease.

Anson's gone.
Kicked off the place he was born on
by somebody he never met.

They were good neighbors. My boy and their boys
played together, rode their bikes up and down the road,
built forts in the woods, fished for trout in the brook,
gave each other courage to make it through a day at school.

Anson spread shit on our garden free of charge,
helped me draw my wood, used to take all three boys
on a sleigh behind his snow machine.
Marie took the boys to Morrisville to the movies.
She was pretty and alive. It was fun
to watch her move across a room.
We never visited all that much but they were good neighbors.

Anson busted his ass over there. It was his home
even if he did have to rent it. He busted his ass
and for nothing.

Everybody says the Boynton place is jinxed,
says nobody can make a go of it over there.
Anson could have if he'd had a break.
It's not the farm that's jinxed; it's farming.
Grain goes up, milk goes down.
The U.S. Secretary of Agriculture has deliberately
conspired against the family farm.
The "name of the game" in Washington is agribusiness,
huge consolidated farms big as Continental Can.
Down there they want the family farm to die.
They want fewer and fewer people to have more and more money.

This is not my fantasy. On February 21st, 1975,
the Associated Press reported that Earl Butz,
Secretary of Agriculture, admitted during a Senate hearing
that he thought the family farm should be "phased out."

Here's Butz again, "Farming isn't a way of life.
It's a way to make a living."
God forbid somebody should see his life and living
as the same thing. What are these idiot neighbors of mine
doing anyway thinking they should love their work?
Don't they know the end of work is money?

Listen, this isn't an issue doesn't concern you.
This issue is the death knell
for what little anarchistic independence is left.
It is oligarchy's fanfare,
and the band plays louder every day.

Every summer Anson had a window box of flowers
near the milkhouse door
and every morning after chores
he watered them and then
with the thumb and forefinger of his calloused hand
he gently, gently plucked
the dying blossoms.

As I was saying, last May, on a Saturday, Anson and Marie
sold out. It was a good day.
Anson's prayers were answered.
He'd asked God not to let it rain.
As the sun came up Norman Pellitier —
the auctioneer —
drove down route 15 and up over the hill
to here and told Marie
to have an hour's worth of junk
to get the people started.

By 10 o'clock trucks lined both sides the road
either way from their house half a mile to ours
and that far the other way too.
It was a farmer's auction, too early in the year
for summer people hunting antiques.
There weren't any antiques anyway.
Marie moved around the crowd forcing a smile and waving
like a maitre d' serving up her life.

There was soda and hot dogs
and kids running around screaming, excited by the crowd.
Edith cried. So did Marie. Anson wanted to but didn't.
The farmers stood around and bid, raising a hand quietly,
nodding a head.
But there weren't any jokes.
They knew they were playing bit parts in a movie
about their own deaths.

At the end of the day Anson had taken in 37,000 dollars
and all that in just machinery and stock.
Everybody said he done real good, real good.
But it wasn't good enough.

Anson's working as a mechanic in Burlington now.
He makes 110 dollars a week for his family of four.
They've got a trailer in a trailer park.
We saw them a couple of months ago.
They said they missed it up here on the hill.

Old Man Pike

Old man Pike was a sawyer at the mill
over in Craftsbury.
He lived just down the road from here.
Every morning he walked six miles through the woods
over Dunn Hill saddle while the sun rose.
He took dinner and supper in the village
then walked home across the mountain in the dark.
Sally Tatro who used to live on my place
would hear him coming through the night, singing.
Sometimes he'd stop to gossip
but mostly she only saw him stride by the window
and disappear.

The old man could have stayed at home,
milked cows, like everybody else,
but he needed an excuse to go and come
through the mountains, every day,
all his life, alone.

Old man Pike didn't believe in the local religion of work,
but out of deference, to his neighbors maybe,
he bowed to it,
placed its dullness at the center of his life,
but he was always sure, because of his excuse,
to wrap it at the edges of his days
in the dark and solitary amblings of his pleasure.

Bill

The Pikes have come a long way down
since the old man walked to Craftsbury
every day all his life to saw boards.
There's only Bill and Arnie left as far as I know
and both of them make only enough to stay drunk.

About five years ago one night in January
I dug Bill out of a snowbank.
It was two in the morning and 30 below.
He'd driven off the road where it crosses Bear Swamp.
He was dead drunk.
In fact, when I waded through the snow to his car
I thought he *was* dead,
and he would have been by morning, of cold or carbon monoxide
if I or someone hadn't come along.
The headlights were on and the radio, and Bill
slumped across the wheel with the motor running.
I banged on the door, opened it,
Bill rolled out, head first, into the snow, like a corpse.
I drug him to my car.
As the snow on his face melted, he woke up a little.
Probably he'd been to Cole's Pond Bottle Club.
It was Saturday night.

I shook him, asked him where he wanted to go.
All he did was point to the village.
I knew when we got to Judevine, he'd point to Hardwick,
then Danville, Newport, Derby, Eden,
on and on like that for days while I drove around the ass end
    of the state
and he sobered up, which would be some time since
he brought the Bud with him.
But the bastard pointed me to Arnie's place without
    the slightest error.

I think blind drunks have homing devices pickled in
    their livers
like the ones in geese.
They don't need to see, only point.
They know where home is.

Arnie was still up, drunk too.
I got him to come out and the two of us drug Bill up
over the rotten porch steps
and into a garbage can of empties.
We made such a racket getting him across the porch
    and into the house
that the blue tick out back started howling.
We dumped him on the living room linoleum and I left.
Nobody said thank-you or good-bye.
In fact, in the years since nobody has ever mentioned
    the incident,
except once down at the garage Bill said " 'lo" to me
and in his eyes there was the look of recognition.

We bought a pig from Bill one spring.
When I went into his rusty trailer to pay him
the place smelled like baby shit.

The railroad's started up again
and Bill's got his old job back
when he's sober.
He still raises pigs I guess although I don't know
since even though his place is only a few miles from here
I haven't been past there in years.

I still see him now and then working on the tracks
or buying beer at the garage
but we never speak.
We don't know each other.

Arnie

Arnie and I harvested Christmas trees three falls together.
Arnie is emaciated and always dirty.
He shaves only on Saturday nights
before he goes to the bottle club.
His face is more wretched than any I have ever seen.
All I remember about those falls together
is how much Arnie knew about the second world war
and how his nose dripped.
He'd stand in the snow and shiver like a popple leaf
and his nose would drip.
He never bothered to wipe it
except maybe two or three times a day
he'd sop it gently
with the back of the glove on his right hand.
He had a filthy, ragged, black and green, Johnson Woolen Mills
            jacket he wore summer and winter.
He stole it from the Mount Mansfield Company
when he worked there on the lifts, which is okay with me
since those Stowe bastards steal more from the likes of Arnie
than the likes of Arnie could ever imagine stealing from them.

Don't get me wrong. Arnie's no saint.
No proletarian archetype.

He's always in court.
Arnie is a bad actor and everybody knows it.
But if we're going to discuss gangsters,
let's talk about the big time,

about Stowe, ski capital of the east.
Stowe: stolen from and supported by the state of Vermont.
The beautiful people's island plunked down
in the middle of the filth and loneliness
that stretches from Maine to Georgia, from top to bottom,
all the way down the Appalachian chain.
Let's talk about the thousands of farms gone under
so nice folks like you can have a place to lie around,
about a state of native slaves hanging around all winter
living off unemployment and welfare
waiting for summer so they can mow your lawn
or paint your house for two and a quarter an hour.

Let's talk about the Vermont Development Department
and the "Beckoning Country," about their photographs
in the New York Times of white houses, red barns,
dirt roads and pretty cows, about why they don't take pictures
of Arnie's house or East Judevine or Hardwick or Island Pond
or a hundred other wretched towns, about why they don't
take pictures of kids with body lice or pictures of old ladies
who freeze to death in their beds. Let's talk about why
the legislators let their neighbors rot while they suck up
to those with money from Boston and New York, about how
four times a year, *Vermont Life* sells a slick, full-color
tumble down the dreamy pit of nostalgia where,
for just a dollar a throw, you can sit wreathed
in an imaginary past.

Let's talk about the guy from Greenwich, Connecticut
with 2000 dollars worth of skis on his car
going down the road past Arnie Pike who makes
2000 dollars a year.

I remember one day — in the fall, I think. It was warm
and we'd eaten lunch and were lying around with our boots off
talking about everything and laughing
and somehow I said, because I am who I am,
"Life's really good, most of the time."
Something like that anyway.
And Arnie began shaking his head slowly and his eyes
got sad and "Naw," he said,
"Naw. Not fer me.
Most athe time it ain't."
Then Arnie raised his head quick,
or as quick as slow Arnie could,
and his face had been transformed.
It was ghoulish, terrifying, as if the gates of hell
had tried to swallow him and he had got away.
Then he bared his rotten teeth and said, slow,
with a grin, while his nose dripped,
"But ah'll survive."

Arnie and the other East Judevine uglies will survive,
in spite of the Mountain Company. They will survive
hidden away from downcountry skiers and the big money.
They will survive, wretchedly, disgustingly,
but they will survive.
And when everybody thinks the gene pool has withered
to a ski bum and his apres ski bunny, then,
unknown to everyone who's supposed to know,
the ways of staying alive will still be known
by a few ugly, stinking outlaws living in shacks
along the banks of the Wild Branch.

I was at Arnie's place just once after I took Bill there
                          that night.
It was only a week before Arnie burnt out.
He always said he never bothered with fuses.
Pennies was just as good and cheaper.
Then he'd laugh and show his ugly teeth.
His place smelled like kerosene.
Nobody ever did know exactly why he burnt out,
but Arnie's no Hermie Newcome. He's too timid.
He didn't light it.
It was either the pot burner or the pennies.
Arnie survived.

It was the time I'm talking about when I was there
drinking beer at Arnie's place that he told me, and this
after knowing him five years, that he always had a doe
down cellar — always — year round.
"Ah don't care nathin' fer the warden. He's afraid
tew caum up here. When Sam Raymond was around he'd turn away.
Hell, he was a outlaw himself.
That's why they made 'im warden."

Arnie went down to Massachusetts for a couple of years
to work in a shoe factory.
I guess he made pretty good money,
but he couldn't stand it down there.

One fall we were cutting trees up on Elmore mountain
when color was still in the hills.
It was a clear day and we were up toward the top of the lot
looking out over the Lamoille valley at Eden mountain
about 40 miles away.
That's when Arnie, Arnie the Wretched, the Ugly, the Stupid,
the Drunk, the Outlaw, the Poor —
that's when Arnie said,
"Lookit 'at. 'At's why ah live here."

And we looked across the ancient green and brown
and red and yellow mountains and the sky was blue
and some fleecy clouds and an osprey hunted the Lamoille
and we stood there while Arnie's nose dripped
and we listened to the wind slip through the spruce trees.

Jimmy

Jimmy is 30, an only child, still lives at home
with his mother and his father and works the farm with them.
I might never have known him if my car hadn't broken down
one time just outside East Judevine. Jimmy stopped
and fixed it. We got to be sort of friends.
I don't see him all that much but when I do
we visit. We like each other.

At first glance Jimmy looks retarded, but he's not;
it's just that he still moves awkward like a boy.
His head is too big for his body
and his dark eyes and hair, his grampa's French,
make his round face seem oddly sunken.
He has two fingers missing from one hand,
an accident on the farm.

Jimmy is a good farmer, better than his father,
but probably he'll spend his life working on the homeplace
and come up to 50 with nothing.
It would be just like his father to die and will the place
to someone else.

When I talk to Jimmy, we always talk about machines.
Jimmy loves machines; he's a good mechanic too,
better than his father.

The one time I saw him dressed up was down at the church
for his uncle's wedding.
He was trying to do the right thing so he walked around
like a tin soldier, a permanent smile pasted on his face.
His fly was down.

When Jimmy talks he holds his hands on edge in the air,
fingers tight together, and moves them in little jerks
from side to side as if
they were fish
trying to swim through grease.
He swallows hard at the end of every phrase.

When you pass him on the road and he waves
he raises his hand flat and forward, fingers still
tight together and his face is stern, almost fearful,
like a Byzantine Jesus offering benediction.

We don't visit all that much but when we do it's hard for me
                    because
there is something I always want to ask him, something
I want to blurt out, drop the talk of carburetors
and say, "Jimmy, what do you do for sex?"

He's 30, lives at home, upstairs, over his parents' room.
There's no woman for him anywhere. He never goes out.
His parents never take him anywhere.
He never sees any of his old high school friends,
if he ever had any.

I want to say, "Jimmy! I want to know. Do you still take
your penis in your hands? How often? Where? In your room
after mother and father have gone to sleep? Do you ride
your snow machine into the woods and do it there?
Don't you want a woman? When you go down to Morrisville
to the feed store where that girl works at the counter,
when you could reach over, touch her breast,
what do you think about?
Is milking cows dawn and dark enough for you?
Is your snow machine enough?
Do you ever dream of something else?

Or maybe you are happy. Maybe you like it there at home.
What's so very wrong with that?

Or is it, Jimmy, in your 30 years you've come to be
a kind of slave, a eunuch,
in the fields of your lord
and father.

Envoy to Jimmy

First I've got to tell you
there's only one radio station around here
anybody ever listens to
because it's the one with the farm news
and the local news and the Trading Post
and comes on at five so folks have music to milk cows by.

Everybody listens to it while they're going down the road.
It's nice because
everybody's head bounces to the same tempo.

I was coming home one day up the river road
and saw Jimmy coming toward me in the pickup
headed for the sawmill or the feed store.

I was going to toot and wave, I always do,
mostly everybody does. Then I saw him
in the cab in that instant
as we passed each other
his arms stretched straight against the wheel,
his head thrown back, eyes almost closed,
his mouth   wide with song.

Antoine

Spring, six years ago.
My first day as a laborer on a Christmas tree farm.
I pulled my pickup to the side of the road,
hopped over a drainage ditch running full
and started up a slope toward a man
standing about a quarter mile away.
Even now, the first of May,
the woods still stood in better than a foot of rotten snow,
but here where the earth tilted south the ground was bare.
Above the grays and browns of last year's matted grass
the young Christmas trees seemed irridescent
in the morning sun.

Antoine stood motionless, watching me come up the hill.

Yew da new mans? Taut yew was. Mike said yew
was caumin'. Ah'm Antoine LaMotte! Ah live alone
ina trailer up on Aiken Pond. Shitagoddamn!
good tu be in da sun again!

He offered me a cigaret and lit us both.

Antoine is a small man, five two or three.
About his cheeks there is that unmistakable alcoholic sheen.
His neck moves in deepening shades of red toward the back until
between his hair line and his collar it is the color
                  of wild strawberries.
His hair is thin but black and his dark eyes dance
when he talks, which he does incessantly.
His whole body moves with the rhythm of his words;
his hands flutter in front of him as if they were
dancing to the music of his speech.
He walks like a duck.
He bangs around the house of his body like a baby.
He is small, featherlight, delicate and infinitely tender.

We stood for a long time smoking, looking out
over the mountains.

Wall! yew mus' be crazy fauckin' basserd take
a job like dis! Bull an' jam like da res' a hus
fer tew an' a korter an'our. Yew crazy as me!
By Chris' an' Saint Teresa don't yew say ah di'in't
warn ya. Before yer dun, yer tongue hang ou',
touch ho' hang daown, yew pull an' tug 'till
yew cas' yer withers. Yer mamma roll over in'er
grave, cry ou', "Oh! by Jesus, how ah fail yew
as a mudder!" Whan yew go hum tanight yer littl'
wimens gonna haf'ta take a raincheck.
She gonna hate yew tanight!
An' yew gonna start tahate these friggin' trees.
Yew gonna wish yer mudder was a baby girl!

Wall, what else is 'ere ta du? No goddamn work
'raound here anymore. Guess yew know dat
else yew weren't be daum enuf ta be 'ere.
Naow! no work. No work atall.
Can't mi'k caows anymore.

Ah yanked does tittys, shauveled dat shit, all mah life,
den they caum an' say ah gots tew haf' a bulk tank
an' can' keep a pig in da barn an' godda wash
mah han's in dis and mah feets in dat julluk ah be
saum kinda brain sergen or suthin'
so ah says shit tu that an' have a nauction
an' ah be glad tu git dun fer 'baout a day.
Den ah begin dreamin' 'baout dem caows and haf'a version.
Ah cud see 'im standin' in der stalls. Mah littl'
gir' friends, an' ah wander 'raound dat empty barn
an' oh! by Jesus, ah wus sick in mah heart!
Nathin' tew do wi' mah days. Nauthin'.
So ah caum crawlin' over here work out
be saumbody else's slave, 'stead a mah own
an' naow ah sleep in one of them friggin' ice boxes
all to mahsef' an' watch some down country somebody
tear daown mah house an' barn what ah was born in shit!
Nathin' tu dew 'raound here nomore.

All da quarries over tu Buffalo Mountain gone.
Stun sheds in Ha'dwick all fallin' daown.
Nathin' over there but rats and crazy ol' Artie Mezey
hidin' in da sheds inside a' ol' car drinkin'
blackberry brandy an' waitin' fer saum littl' boys
ta caum along. Chris'! da whole goddamn taown
jes' fallin' in da reever. Ah! whan ah was a boy
it weren't dat way. Dey was mills an' bars.
Thuty-tew bars in dat littl' place!
Have good times der tew, wall ah guess!
Good whore house too. Ah used ta go confession
over to the church on Friday afternoon
den step across da street take in a littl' matinee.
Da church still der but da whore house she ain't.

When da sheds close daown dat taown shrivel
like a moldy squash. Nathin' left.

On'y saum ol' Wop cutters, ones still livin',
what can't go out winners 'cause a da hair, stayin' ta hum
coughin' out der lungs. Ah! wada yew care!

There was an embarrassed silence.
Then he went on.

Wall, here we be, ain't we? No more sittin'
by da stof 'till Doc say yew be dun.
Shitagoddamn, goddamnashit, dis da right place ta be
caum spring, bull and jam 'raound here outin da sun
thin yer blood. Don't need no tonic here, shitacatsass naow!
Ol' Doc give us a tonic. Couple weeks walkin'
twenty miles a day spredin' this fauckin' fert'lizer
an' yer blood'll be runnin' good. Rock. Jus' rock
ya know. That's what we're spreddin' all day long;
15-10-10 an' wha's da odder sistyfife? Rock!
'nert 'greedients is what dey try ta tellya
but don' yew beliefit, Mister Man, it's rock,
peacestone, from the mine, groun' up fine. Gee Wiss,
Gee Wiss Chris'! ya'd tink a man a 45 do suthin' sides
sprinkle rock onto baby trees. Hell, comeon.
Ah'llgetjabucket.

We set off down the hill toward a tractor and a wagon
piled with 80 pound bags of Red Fox fertilizer.

When I first knew Antoine he drank a lot,
a sixpack for breakfast on the way to work,
then another couple during the day.
I'm sure he drank himself to sleep.
But he never missed work and he never drank anything
but beer. He swore that if you drank only beer
you'd never become an alcoholic.

Ah'm no alacholic. Not like Uncle Clyde. He got
an alacholic tumor big as a cabbage in his stomach.
Got tu feed it brandy ever' day.
Me, ah ain't nathin' but a goddamn drunk.
Alacholism fer dem multitude millionaires. Politicians.
Per fauckin' basserds da likes a me jus' goddamn drunks.

David, yew like politics? Ah watch dat news
'baout ever' night. Watch them crazy basserds
jomp araound. Goddamn multitude millionaires.
Gangsters. Any of 'em wuth a turd get a bullet
in the head. All them Kennedys and that Martin
Luther King. Oh Jesus! how ah love dat junglebunny!
He like me, radder be a lover dan a fi'der.
See how far it got 'im! Naow! whiteman da biggest basserd
whatever live. Steal da country from da Indians
then make da niggers do da work. Wall, people's mean
all over. Up here iss Skinheads 'gainst da Frogs.
Ah know what they call me an' ah don' care.
Let 'em call me what dey want if that's the way
they get der pleasure. Elwin tol' me what Alfreda said
'baout me not havin' no more brains 'an a frog's got feathers.
Wall, she got peasoup in 'er veins tew! Hell, whada ah care.
Nigger ahda Nord, tha's me, an' ah don' care.
Poof! ah know plenty. Ah jus' can' t'ink of it.
Ah seen frogs she never with han's big as hams,
once I even seen a snake with legs up on Stannard Mountain
but shit if ah ever see a frog with feathers.
Jus' 'cause she marry a skinhead drunk she t'ink herse'f
better 'an 'er gra'ma. She eat dem lags tew.
Hell tu her! Yew get yerse'f a bran sack full, skin 'em easy,
roll 'em in flar, salt an' pepper, fry 'em quick,
haf' a couple beers and by Jesus yew got suthin' good.

Then Antoine met Shirley.
They lived together in a trailer up in Collinsville
     with her two boys.

About a month after all of us knew what was going on,
Antoine finally said,

David! got me a wimens! Workin' out, tew.
Workin' out good. 230 pounds and not an ounce
a fat. Caum up here from Joisy. Dat's how she talk.
Dat's how she say it. Shitacatsass, ain't dat funny?
Ah! it make me laf da way she talk. She good wimens.
Ah'd marry her tamarra if it weren't we loose
da welfare an' her wid them two outlaw boys.
Mah rockin' chair money ain't enauf. Was fer me,
get me tru da winner, but ain't fer four a hus.
If we be on'y tew, be okay, but she got dem bad actin' saverges.
Shitagoddamn, if we be on'y tew . . .
Wall, better'n livin' to mahse'f in dat trailer
wi' nathin' but mah goddamn dawg.

It lasted about a year.
Then Shirley left, went down to a place in Barre.

David, she lef' me. Walk right aout. Poof!
Ah back in dat trailer wi' dat friggin' dawg.
On'y frien' ah got. Tew friggin dawgs.
Alone again. Jus' like that goddamn Raymond.
Ah! goddamnit ta shit, what's the use!
Piss on dat fire. Les' go drink saum bier.
Comeon, David, drink bier wi' me.
Les' go drink saum bier.

I didn't go and I've been sorry ever since.
Antoine began missing more and more work until he was
                             showing up about once a week.
That's when Bert fired him.
About a month after Antoine got fired he came over to my place
one Saturday afternoon. He was filthy. His eyes were beets.
He hadn't shaved in weeks.
He had a quart of Schaeffer in his hand.

Dawyd, how yu be? Ah ain't tu good. Fawk,
ah'm 'cinegratin', Dawyd. Caumin' apart tew pieces.
Don' know wha' ah gonna dew. I di'in't know ah luf
dat wimens so. Ah di'in't know it. Mah mamma she
be right. Ah Chris', ah wish she be a baby girl.

I didn't see Antoine for another couple months.
Then, again on a Saturday afternoon, he showed up,
clean clothes and shaven. He looked like his old self,
only better.

David! shit a cat's ass, we back together!
Naow yew better si' daown.
Dis gonna get yew in da stomach,
right between da shoul'er blaze.
David, ah gonna be a fadder!
By Chris', ah never taut it caum tew be.
Oh, my mamma be so pleaze. She die t'inkin'
she fails me as a mudder, t'ink ah end mah days
a smelly bach'er drunk. Dah las' time midnight
New Year's Eve ah caum in kneel at mah fadder,
da year he die, ah be turdy den, an get da blessin'
when he puts his han' on mah head an says da words
ah know he a'mos' cry 'cause he know he dyin' and he know
ah spen' mah days yankin' mah tool an' spillin' mah seed.
Now dat littl' wimens got me growin' in 'er an'
Oh by Jesus, ah be happy as a puppy to da roa'!
Oh! ah wish tu hell ah cud marry her!
She caum hum from docter's, si' daown a' da table,
tell me, we bod' cry all af'ernoon, be so happy.
Nex' day ah go to docter's say you he'p me naow
ah can' be drunk no more, ah gonna be a fadder.
He say ah be alacholic, ah say Naow! how dat be!
Ah taut nobody be alacholic what drink on'y beer.
Thas why ah never drink da har' stuff. He say naow ah am!
Ah di'in't know it! Shitagoddamn, all dah years me t'ink

ah nathin' but a goddamn drunk ah be high class alacholic
julluk da Presedent.
He say ah quit or ah never see mah baby grow
and by Jesus dat t'ree weeks ago an ah ain't pull a ring
since. An' ah ain't gonna tew neider. We gonna name 'im
Pierre and if he be a girl, Michelle. Shitagoddamn, David,
naow ah be like you goddamn bookwriters, ah got mah head
in da clouds, no more on da graoun' dan da moon,
an' Doc gimme mah job back tew. Ah tol' 'im
ah got mah reason tew work naow. Fauck me!
Ah'll pick bluebird shit off da white cliffs a Dover
if ah haf' tew.

Shirley had the baby and Antoine stomped around
like a banty rooster.
Then it was spring again.

Graoun's a bullin', David. Time ta plant da seed.
Yew got tew make yer wedder. Got tew du it naow.
Jes' da right time. It's mudder nature. Like a wimens.
You be like me las' year, cabbage an' tomato
gone ta hell but ah get a sidehill a patada
 an' a baby girl. Dis year Poppa gonna plow
da whole goddamn state for his gardin.

Oh Jesus, ah a'mos' fergot, dat hippy girl live up da roa'
caum over see da baby. She lean over coo,
her tittys hangin' daown loose
so big dey weren't fid a sap bucket
an' ah see her pussy tew stickin out her pants
big a' witches broom. Bah! how ah wish
ah be dat littl' baby. Hell, an ol' buck got a stiff horn
an' ah ain't be dun yet!

Shit, David, we got tu get onmarried from these goddamn trees!
Ah'm sick of it!

Ah'm goin' home. Two o'clock an' ah don't care. Ah'm goin' tu da matinee. Ah be! Ah got tu see dat wimens and mah little baby.
Yew tell Doc ah ain't functionatin' right today. Tell 'im ah be back tamarra.

Bobbie

For years Bobbie drove the pickup truck to Morrisville
every day to sew the flys in men's pajamas at a factory
down there. When you spoke to her about the job,
she'd blush and turn on her heel like a little girl.
She was good. The best one down there.
It was piece work and she was fast.
She quit the sewing when she and Doug went to farming.

Bobbie is beautiful, or could be.
Under thirty years of work and plainness you can see
her body, see her face,
those definite, delicate features
glowing.
She strides like a doe.
In spite of two brown teeth
her smile is warm and liquid.

Last summer she cut off a finger in the baler,
paid her farmer's dues.

Now she holds her missing finger behind her when she talks.
She's got something new to blush for.

Doug

Last summer Doug pastured horses down at Sally Tatro's
in the village. He had eight down there.
One of the two big workhorses, the mare of the team,
got an apple stuck in her throat. When Doug found her
she was lying in a swamp almost dead from suffocation.
Doug skidded her out of the wet place with his pickup.
Then he called the vet.

"Doc Jeffers come up, said the only thing to do was shoot her.
I asked him if he'd do it. He said no.
I asked Roy and Jerry. Nobody would.
So I come got my gun and did it myself.
After I done it, I sat down and bawled like a baby.
We logged together two winters."

What Doug didn't tell me but what I found out later
was that after he killed the mare, he stayed with her
all that afternoon and into the dark of that night.
He stayed with her until her eyes clouded, until
she got cold.

Doug's better than six feet, weighs more than 300 pounds.
He has a couple of teeth missing up front and his voice

is high and pinched. It doesn't belong to his body.
When Doug laughs he sticks his enormous stomach out,
throws his head and shoulders back and laughs loud,
with his mouth open, like a picture I saw once
of a Russian peasant in *The Family of Man*.

Until recently Doug jumped from job to job
never keeping one more than a couple of months.
But he always had work. People hated him for that,
and for his saying,
"I try not to work too much in the winter.
Gets in the way of my snow machinin'."
Like Edith says, "Shiftless bum's what he is. On'y thing
he ever done regalar is eat."

Doug has cut logs and pulp, worked at the Firestone store
in Barre, been a mechanic in Burlington, worked for the
highway and the railroad, been a farmer, a carpenter,
hauled used brick, sold barn boards and beams, trucked gravel,
pumped gas, driven a school bus, cut brush at Christmas time
and worked on the lifts for the Mountain Company and all that
in the six years I've known him.
He's never been fired. He always quits.

Doug worked on the lifts when Arnie did.
They drove to work together; 80 miles a day round trip
so they could stand on top the state
and freeze their asses for a buck and a half an hour;
all day on top the mountain bowing and smiling,
helping New York ladies off the lifts.

Doug told me once how they got the turkeys.
As the chair topped the rise, they'd reach out,
offer the skier a hand.
That was their job.
Then, at just the right moment, give a little jerk
and down the turkey would go.

"Oh! pardon me ma'am! Excuse me! You alright?
Then we'd help her up, grab a little pussy or a tit,
get her going, step on the back of a ski and down
                she'd go again.

"Jerry Willey worked up there with us too, that little dink.
All he ever talked about was gettin' in their pants.
Used to say he'd grab one, get her down
stick her skis in the snow, stake her
so she couldn't get away, and fuck her,
bang away, right there, 5000 feet in the air.
Then he'd say, 'I'd climb offin her an' say,
"Okay, rich lady, now les' see you get down that mountain."'

"All Jerry ever talked about was gettin' a rich piece of ass.
Said he'd heard it smelt differ'nt, said all them ladies
wear silk underpants and spray their cunts with peach perfume.
Well, I'll tell you this, I don't think it smells no differ'nt;
              do you?
But I'd like to know myself. Seen plenty of 'em up there
I wouldn't mind tryin' out. But I never did, and Jerry
never did neither.
That's a differ'nt class naow, ain't it?
Pussy in a silk sack. Peach pussy. Imagine that!"

After Granny died Doug and Bobbie started farming her
              old place.
But the milk check is too small.
They can't get by on only cows.
Unemployment's up to 15% and Doug doesn't find jobs
the way he used to.

The last time I saw him he looked serious and sad.
He asked me, *me*, if I knew of any work.
I haven't seen him throw his stomach out,
his head and shoulders back and laugh
in a long time.

Envoy to Doug

Doug told me once
he always wanted to go to college
study, get a certificate,
be a math teacher
in a school somewhere.
He likes kids. Everybody knows that.

We've got a new roller rink down in Morrisville now
and it turns out Doug's the best one there.
Six foot, three hundred pounds, the biggest pot
you've ever seen, but he moves across the floor
so light it seems he isn't even touching.
He can skate backwards, do a spin.

When he and Bobby start to dance
everybody watches. They glide and twirl.
Bobby smiles her shy smile
then Doug draws away on one skate,
a loop, a spin, alone across the floor.
You can hear his squeaky laugh rise
above the noise of skate wheels and organ.

He spreads his arms and legs apart
and floats across the floor smooth
as cream, his body open, leaning
on the air.

Granny

Granny lived down the road from Albert.
She was 80 when she died. Everybody said she was crazy.
Probably she was. She was suspicious of everyone.
She had visions, saw conspiracies, thought every stranger
who came along was out to get her.
She always liked me because I waved when I went by.

Granny had a cleft palate and no teeth.
She was also hard of hearing
so when she talked to you she shouted.
Her husband died about ten years ago.
The winter he died the house burnt down.
Granny spent the last decade of her life alone
living in a springhouse and a camper trailer.
She milked ten cows every day, twice a day, to the day
she died.
She was obsessed with the memory of her husband, Lee.
She talked about him constantly
and when she did
she moaned a nasal, toothless, hairlipped moan.

Granny had a dream of selling out, moving
to Morrisville to manage an apartment building.

She lived her dream and sold her place about twice a year.
She'd have a lawyer draw a deed and bill of sale,
then at exactly the last moment, she'd back out.
Nobody ever had the heart, thank God, to make her follow through.
Everybody understood how Granny was.

Once a guy from Hardwick
who didn't know what buying land from Granny really meant
actually got a cattle truck of Holsteins to the barn.
The neighbors could see what was coming
so we stopped by to watch the show.
The guy climbed down out of the cab all smiles.
Granny was waiting for him, the bill of sale in her hand.
She hollered something at him about her husband,
then lit the bill of sale and threw it at him.
After that she didn't sell the place so much.

Granny couldn't leave. The day the house burnt down
Lee's ghost left the house and went to living in the barn.
She couldn't leave Lee's ghost.

Granny never did anybody any harm.

A few years ago, in August, after haying,
a woman we had met at a party in Craftsbury came to see us.
She had a kid with her, a guy about 18.
They were driving an old Pontiac station wagon.
There were four dogs in the back.
They parked at the foot of the drive.
The car's shocks were gone and even after they got out,
the car still bobbed and shivered in its place
like a tin behemoth with Parkinson's disease.

They staggered up the hill to the house.
They were high or drunk or both.

It was 10 o'clock in the morning.
We drank some of their wine; then they drove off
down the road toward the village.

Later I found out they stopped at Granny's place.
Granny was in the pasture
graining a heifer she had staked under a maple tree.
They jumped out of the car
and ran across the pasture to the old woman.
She was a total stranger to them.
They hugged her and kissed her and shouted wildly,
"Power to the People! Power to the People!"
They told Granny they were going to give her lots of money
and that she'd never have to work again.
Granny broke away from them and ran into the barn
and hid in the hayloft. Bobbie found her up there
that evening after dark.

The woman from Craftsbury and her friend came back
once more that summer.
This time Granny was in the barn when they pulled up.
She ran out the back, across the pasture, through a swamp
and hid in the high grass of Rufus Chaffee's orchard
all afternoon.

Granny died last spring, in the morning
while she was doing chores.
Bobbie found her about noon, lying in the gutter,
the milking machine still pulsating in her hand
and the cows blatting from the pain of stretched udders.

I miss Granny. I miss her angry voice.
I miss her plaintive wail for Lee.

I remember the first time I ever met Granny.
I was bucking firewood one fall, some maples

the power company had let down
along the lane into Uncle Clyde's.
Granny shuffled over from her trailer on the hill.
She was furious.

"'ut 'er 'ooin! 'ew 'ow 'ut 'er 'ooin?
'ems 'ah 'ees! 'oo'ol'ew'ew 'ou'd 'ut 'em?
'ut 'er 'ooin! 'ems 'ah 'ees!
'iss 'ah 'an', ain't 'yde's!
I 'ew 'ief 'ee?
Ah'm an ol' 'oman, 'even'y-'ix 'ears ol'
'ah 'us'un's 'ead. 'ah 'oaus 'urnt ou'.
'ah 'if a'on i'a 'ing'oaus an a 'ailer,
'ah 'ik 'en 'aows.
'ah əh 'et i!"

I apologized. Told her I didn't mean to steal her trees.
Said I thought they were Clyde's. Granny mellowed
and ended telling me I was welcome to the wood.

"'er 'el'um 'ew 'at 'ood.
ah'm 'ad 'er 'ew 'ew 'ave ih.
Ih 'ew 'eed ih, ah'm 'ad 'er 'ew 'ew 'ave ih.
'er 'ik'd on 'iss 'ill. Ah 'een'ew 'o i.
'ew 'ave.
'er 'ik'd on 'iss 'ill.
Ah'm 'ad 'er 'ew 'ew 'ave ih."

Then she began about her husband, Lee.
It was the first time I'd ever heard her lament.
Her vowels elongated. She lengthened all her final sounds,
syncopated all her phrases. She moaned. She wailed.
She rolled her head and sang.

"Oh, ah 'ish   'ew'd 'et   ah 'us'un', 'ee!
'ee uz ah 'icest 'an   'at e'er 'od   in 'ews!

'ee um 'alkin' 'oun ah 'oad   un 'ay,   'opped in
'an 'e'er 'eft.
'ow 'e's 'ead!
Ah 'us'un's 'ead!
An' ah'm an ol' 'oman,   'even'y-'ix 'ears ol',
ah 'us'un's 'ead!
Ah 'oaus 'urnt ou',
ah 'if a'on i'a 'ing'oaus an a 'ailer,
ah 'ik 'en 'aows,
ah əh 'et i!

Ah 'us'un's 'ead!
'ee's 'ead!

an ah'm   a'oun!

Forrest

Forrest died five years ago.
I never knew him.
But I saw him, almost daily, winter and summer,
flapping down the Dunn Hill road to the family graves
up where Hermie used to live.

I could see him loping
taking those huge strides as if he were
angrily running after
a child,
his old gray overcoat dragging
on the gravel

and that world war one
aviator's hat
flapping
at his ears.

Requiem for a Hill Farm

Raymond died last spring.
Or was it 50 springs ago?
It doesn't matter.
It was spring.
It is always spring.

A warming day. Winter's back
broken. Light rising.
He quit. Gave up
the ghost. Left
a withered carcass slumped
across the kitchen table.

With the man gone
the place dies
like an old pine dying
bit by bit, from tips
inward. The outward sign
of inner forgotten death.

The garden goes to witchgrass, timothy,
aster, hardhack,
gray birch, red maple.

Balsam, spruce begin
their long reach through the roof
of his old car.

One night coyote sits
on Raymond's porch
and howls: notice to the rest:
this again
is nowhere.

Mullein grows
midroad.

The roof lets in rain.
Joists buckle, floors warp,
rafters groan and sag.
All give up geometric pretense,
go pulpy soft.

Chimney brick dilapidates.
Someone steals the windows.
Porcupines come in.

The house fills with quills and shit.

Two dead porkys in the sink.
The sofa is a nesting bird's delight.
A broken chair.

Then down.
Disheveled nest.
Pile of sticks.
There is no in   no out.

Raspberries sprout from Raymond's
sodden mattress.

What boards are left turn black.

Albert

Like Edith says, "Albert Putvain's a no good wuthless pup,
ain't too swift neither.
When he was clearin' lan' 'raound his trailer
he c'ught the corner of the place wi' the crawler blade
an' tore the bedroom off.
But that ain't nathin', when he was young he an' his brother
                            was workin' in the woods
an' Albert backed a crawler right up over top his brother,
squashed 'im flat, killed 'im,
an' it ain't never seemed ta bother Albert any.

"Why, he don't know when ta quit.
Him 65 and a fifth wife an' a baby girl.
Why, he's got kids from here ta Brattleboro.
Prab'ly the on'y thing he ever learned ta dew
so he jes' keeps doin' it.

"An' those tew ol' state guys he boards up in that ol' bus,
poor re-tards,
they'd be better off back daown to the hospital,
an' Albert sayin',
'Ah mik 'im walk da woads so dey won't git wazy.'
Why, yew know he's makin' money off that thing,

yew know he is.
Albert knows more ways a makin' money doin' nathin'
'an the whole res' athe worl' put together.
But they c'ught 'im tew, didn't they?
Last year, one week, got convicted 13 times
a welfare frawd."

Albert is also an architect.
He has garnished his trailer, as many people do,
with porches and sheds and leantos and a garage
so that now you can't even see the trailer
it's so buried in the rubble of his invention.

He has an old hay knife painted silver suspended from wires
hanging over the garage door and a silver sickle and a
silver milk can with a gilded colonial eagle perched
on top of it. In the dooryard there is a whorl
of flower pots with plastic red and white carnations
hanging from the tines of an old hay rake.
Watching over all of this are six pink flamingos
on wire legs, each standing and nodding in the wind.
And out front, perpendicular to the road
so you can see it good,
there's a hand painted sign that glows in the dark
and says:
                MR. PUTVAIN.

The Two Old Guys at Albert's

There are two retarded guys from the State Hospital
boarded in a bus at Albert's. I don't know their names.
Nobody does. Albert never takes them anywhere.
Maybe the state told him not to; I don't know.
It's not much. An old bus to sleep in, nothing to do
but walk the road and shovel snow, bounce a ball
for Albert's kid in the afternoon, listen to each other
masturbate at night. Not much, but better than the hospital.

The ward   a room   crowded with 50 beds
25 on either wall.   The old men who lie   all day
on their sides   all facing   the same way
so no one has to face   another.   Their only cooperation.
The old men who lie   all day   and say   nothing
look at   nothing.   The kid   14   who rocks all day
in a chair   that doesn't rock.   Cold coffee
from a peanut butter jar.   The smell of men
who wet their pants.   Stale tobacco air.   Dark halls.
And doors   locked doors.   The moans at night.
And once a day   the doctor
with a hypodermic.

The manic girl   across the courtyard   who every day
takes down her pants   and dances   jangling
like a crow   across the porch   crying   like a crow
"Hey Baby!   Hey Baby!   Come over here!"
She lifts her dress   and puts   fingers
between her legs   and rubs   twitching   like a crow
until she falls   her wings spread out   her body
shivering   on the porch floor.

You   watching   through the window   your penis
in your hands   in a room with 50 others
rubbing   rubbing   while you watch   and while
the attendant   watches you.
Then your hand is sticky   smelling of ammonia.
You wipe it on your pants   front and back
strop it   like a razor.

I have seen men jailed in rooms   all of them   so lost
so alone   that there is nothing —
not a summer rain   not a smile   not a doughnut —
to be shared. Men like particles of dust   suspended
in the air   floating wantonly   at random   making
accidentally   without purpose   action and reaction
to no end   men   (like me)   moving   isolated
dumb   unknowing   suspended in the air.

There are these two retarded guys boarded up at Albert's.
You can see them every day walking the road between
their bus and where the hill starts up to Granny's.

The younger one, who looks about 15 but probably is 40,
tilts and limps as he walks. His mouth
is permanently distorted and his misshapen head shows
that if he ever had a mother
she didn't care enough to roll him in his crib
so his head wouldn't flatten in the back.

When I wave to him he jerks his arm up, stops
turns his ugly face and smiles.
Then quick, as if someone hollered at him,
he goes on walking,
tilting and limping and walking.

I wonder if he dreams about the manic girl,
if he still sees her in the night,
jangling in her bones, dancing, crying for him
like a crow.

The older one who looks, and probably is, 55
walks straight but keeps his arms out from his sides
stiff and at an angle.
His hands flutter constantly.
When I wave to him his roadside arm rises and falls,
rises and falls,
with the hand fluttering at its end,
but his eyes stay down on the road.
I have never seen his face.
The old guy keeps that up, the arm rising and falling,
the hand trembling at its end.
I can see it in the rear view mirror until I make the bend.

There are two retarded guys boarded up at Albert's.
Every day they walk the road.
They never walk together.
They are always
about a hundred feet apart.

Tom

Tom spent 18 months in Vietnam. Pleiku, Hue.
Names, strange, not at all like Judevine.
He was a hero when he got home.
Folks around here were proud of him, or if they weren't
they didn't say so. He had done his duty
and that was that.
Don't doubt it. It is true.
Everybody tried to make him feel at home
in his home. Some said he was nervous;
he had changed. Or maybe it was they
who moved around him circling at a distance
like dogs around a bear, wondering
what it was was in their midst.

When deer season came, Tom got his deer,
as he had always done, every year, since he was twelve.
He was the greatest hunter on the hill
and now everybody knew he was somehow even greater.
One shot dropped his buck, as always, and,
as always, as the seven times before,
he dressed his deer in the accustomed way,
opening the belly from sternum to vent,

his knife slipping cleanly through the hide and flesh.
Then a new maneuver.

His knife rung the genitals, extracting penis
and the testicles and with them a tab of belly skin.
He hung them by the fleshy ribbon in a tree
just as he had done
in Vietnam.

When the people heard of it, the men snickered and said
they'd have to try that next year
and the circle widened and we moved at a distance,
like dogs around a bear, wondering
what it was was in our midst.

Driving Home at Night

Midnight. Outside the car it is
15 below. A foot of new snow.
The village is deserted, dark,
except for eight street lamps
and the light in the window
at Jerry's Garage that says:
BEER.

The smell of woodsmoke seeps
into the car.

Judevine, ugliest town
in northern Vermont, except
maybe East Judevine.
Disheveled, wretched, Judevine —
my town — is beautiful
in the night.

It is beautiful because
its couple hundred souls
have given up their fears,
their poverty and worry.
For a few hours now they know
only the oblivion of sleep
and the town lies quiet
in their ease.

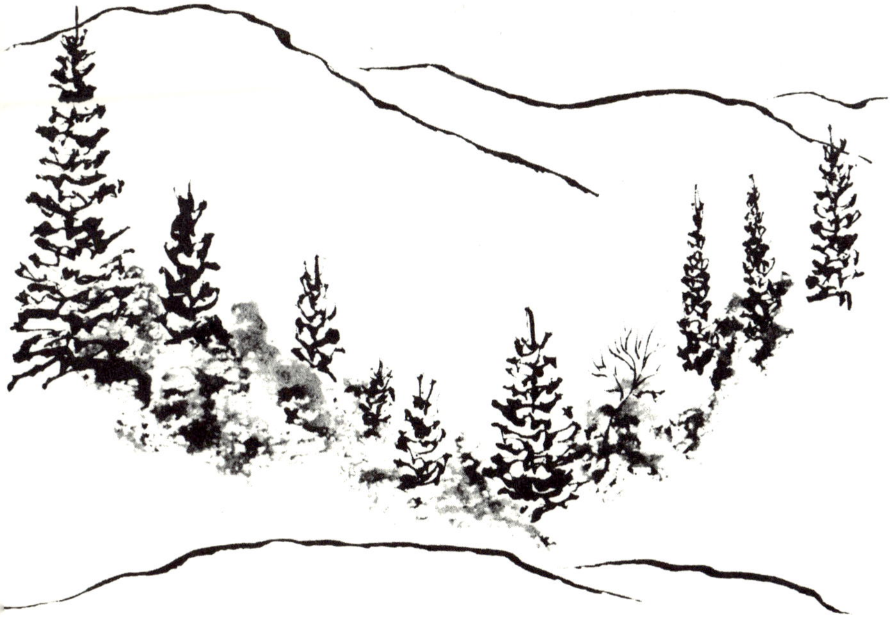

Appendix: Literal Transcription of Granny's Monologues

What you doing! You know what you're doing?
Them's my trees! Who told you you could cut them?
What you doing! Them's my trees!
This my land, ain't Clyde's!
Why you grief me?
I'm an old woman, seventy-six years old.
My husband's dead. My house burnt out.
I live alone in a springhouse and a trailer.
I milk ten cows.
I just get by!

* * *

You're welcome to that wood.
I'm glad for you to have it.
If you need it, I'm glad for you to have it.
You're liked on this hill. I seen you go by.
You wave.
You're liked on this hill.
I'm glad for you to have it.

* * *

Oh, I wish   you'd met   my husband, Lee.
He was the nicest man   that ever trod   in shoes.
Lee come walking down the road   one day   stopped in
and never left.
Now he's dead!
My husband's dead!
And I'm an old woman,   seventy-six years old
my husband's dead.
My house burnt out,
I live alone in a springhouse and a trailer,
I milk ten cows,
I just get by!

My husband's dead!
Lee's dead!

And I'm   alone!